# of books, stones, friends and visions

edited by Adam Stout

two rivers press 1997

Published in 1997 by Two Rivers Press.

ISBN 1901677 036

Designed and typeset on the RISC apple mac by Pip Hall and output on a laserjet printer.

Printed by Watkiss Sudios Limited Biggleswade, Bedfordshire.

contents

For, indeed, the greatest glory of a building is not in its stones, nor in its gold. Its glory is its Age, and in that deep sense of voicefulness, of stern watching, of mysterious sympathy, nay, even of approval or condemnation, which we feel in walls that have long been washed by the passing waves of humanity.

John Ruskin *The Seven Lamps of Architecture*

George Lovejoy, former occupant of this building, refused all payment for the loan of any of Ruskin's books from his circulating library, claiming their value was so great that no money payment would be adequate.

introduction

London Street is Reading's most beautiful road. 'This is a street with a very definite power to charm', wrote Arthur Henry Anderson in 1906, and he praised 'its ample breadth, its slow, deliberate curve and gentle slope, and the wonderful admixture of varying but charmingly harmonised styles of building. It is an odd medley of architecture, yet there is a mellowness and richness that make London Street really notable'. Godwin Arnold, perceptive architectural historian of this town, once described London Street as 'one of the pleasures of living in Reading'.

That was in 1968, just before the road-builders got to work on the Inner Distribution Road. London Street remains attractive, but the IDR severed it from the town centre, with predictable results. Shops closed, buildings deteriorated. Planning blight set in, the For Sale signs proliferated, and London Street seemed doomed. The *Evening Post* once called it 'Reading's Street of Shame'.

Things are slowly changing now, and one of the catalysts for change has been Reading International Solidarity Centre. RISC moved to number 103, at the top of the street, in 1987. Now, ten years later, they have re-opened in the street's most famous building: the London Street Bookshop.

RISC occupies three adjacent buildings: 35, 37 and 39 London Street (119, 118 and 117 respectively before the street was re-numbered in the 1870s: to avoid confusion

we have used the modern numbering throughout.) All three are listed, and although it seems unlikely that any of the buildings now standing predates the eighteenth century, they all incorporate building materials that are older, and were almost certainly taken from previous buildings on the same site. Why buy in a new beam, or a load of stone, when there's good enough to be found on site? The result is a

complicated mish-mash of bits and pieces from every peri-
od. Working out what was built when, and for whom, and
above all why, is what this book tries to
do. We're bound to have got at least
some of it wrong, so apologies upfront to
future sleuths and historians who discover
our mistakes.

If buildings have souls, then the souls of
these three are in good shape. This is a
warm and friendly place. Even the ghost
is benign, and it is uncanny how RISC's
humanitarian aims were shared by former occupants.

A group of the pacifist Society of Friends (Quakers) met here between
1692 and 1715; they left the main body because they supported such caus-
es as women's' rights. Their members included William Penn, founder of
Pennsylvania, who tried to enshrine fair dealings with native Americans
into his new State's constitution. Quaker connections with these premises
continued into the nineteenth century, and the affable and philanthropic
peace-maker George Lovejoy had his famous Bookshop at no. 39.

This booklet is designed to make links and connections between the
past and the future, and to commemorate the Final Official Launch of the
RISC endeavour on Friday 17 October 1997. It is also a chance for us to
thank all the many volunteers and supporters for making it all possible.

Many thanks to Ken Major and H. Godwin Arnold, architectural histori-
ans, and Peggy Drury, social historian, for examining the structure and
sharing their observations; to Joan Dils for kindly passing on details of
two sixteenth-century Reading wills; to Douglas LaPorte and David
Hutchings, formerly of the London Street Bookshop, for their recollec-
tions; to Barry De Lacey Nelson for sharing his vast knowledge of nine-
teenth-century Reading; to Mr and Mrs Smart of the London Street
Research Group for
much useful informa-
tion; and to Rhys
Trussler for interview-
ing RISC's ancient
resident. The errors
are all our own work,
but don't sue, because
we haven't got any
money.

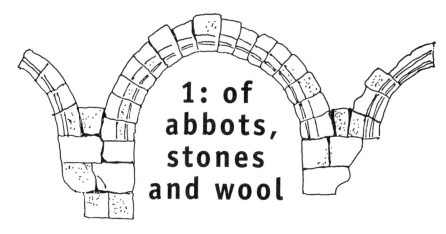

1: of abbots, stones and wool

Old Reading is a town of two halves. The eastern part centres around St Laurence's Church and the Market Place; the western part, around St Mary's Church in the Butts.

The western town is the earliest, and grew up along the main north-south route from Winchester and Southampton through to Oxford. Castle Street, the main road west, begins opposite St Mary's Church, and until King's Road was built in 1833 London-bound travellers had to pass up Southampton Street and turn left along Crown Street and London Road. Unless, that is, they went up London Street.

London Street short-circuits that route. It runs from London Road up to the Market Place and what was once the gate of Reading Abbey; and all the signs are that it was developed by the Abbey as a deliberate piece of town-planning. The first reference to London Street itself comes soon after 1240; but the High Bridge, which connected the Abbey to London Street, is mentioned in 1186, just 22 years after the Abbey itself was formally dedicated.

New town developments of this kind were quite common in the Middle Ages, and in the case of Reading the Abbey's aim was clear. In addition to the revenue that the new burgage (leasehold) plots would bring, they hoped to move

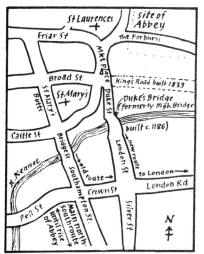

map of Reading before 1833

the town's centre of gravity from St Mary's to a development that – in every sense – was under the shadow of the Abbey.

London Street is a very wide road, and the best explanation for this is that it was originally laid out for a market. (Those who knew the street before the IDR was built point out that the approach to the High Bridge was actually much narrower: this was probably because this portion of the street was within the Kennet flood-plain). Medieval London Street featured a Fair Cross, which may have served as a focus for buying and selling, and when the Abbot tried to move the corn-market from its traditional site in the old town, he quite possibly hoped to move it to London Street. The townspeople were not best pleased, and the incident seems to have triggered off a ten-year quarrel between town and Abbey, culminating in a Concord of 1254 which, amongst much else, restored the corn-market to its former site.

The pull of the Abbey was hard to resist, however. Over the next century Reading's commercial centre drifted inexorably towards the new town. London Street prospered accordingly, and soon became a centre for the cloth trade, Reading's major industry. On the south bank of the Kennet, by the High Bridge, stood the town-wharf with the wool-beam, where the wool was weighed before being despatched down-river. Robert le Taillour (tailor) was an early resident of London Street, with a 'capital messuage' (a large dwelling with adjoining buildings and lands) in 1287, and the street remained a popular address for wealthy clothiers into the sixteenth century.

The very name of London Street indicates that the Abbot intended their new road to become the main route for traffic bound for the capital, but in this he was only partly successful.

The hero of Thomas Deloney's fictitious Thomas Coles of Reading (1602) was a wool-merchant who had a 'great number of Waines loaden with cloth comming to London'. His wagons began their journey in Reading, and there's a good chance that they left the town along London Street. (Coles came to an untimely end in the 'mighty great caldron' of a dastardly Colnbrook innkeeper, but that's another story).

Travellers from further afield, however, would probably have used the old road along Southampton Street and through the Butts. The town's biggest inns (the Crown, and the Bear by Seven Bridges, now Bridge Street, first mentioned in 1483) were to be found along the old road, which indicates that most through traffic preferred to use this route. It continued to do so until the nineteenth century. Stage-coach traffic using London Street and its inns generally terminated in the town; those going on to Bath and Bristol used the old road past the Butts.

The most likely explanation for this is that the Abbot's 'new town' had become so successful that those without particular business in Reading chose to bypass the congestion of Broad Street. The Cheese Fair and the shambles, or butchery, were held at the eastern end of Broad Street, and were replaced by two narrow streets that survived until the 1860s, although it was said 'two carriages cannot pass at a time in either of them';

Minster Street, the alternative route, was in 1648 chained off ('pedestrianised'?) to prevent rat-running by waggons that had presumably come rumbling down London Street.

It thus appears that London Street in the later middle ages had only a limited amount of through traffic, while the markets for which it was probably designed slowly moved closer to the Abbey and to Broad Street across the Kennet. This doesn't mean that the street had 'failed', however: far from it. If anything, it was a rather fashionable suburb, full of the houses of the town's leading merchants and citizens. Here, in 1258, was the messuage of Nicholas the Clerk; here, in 1315, resided William le Cork(er): the Vintners' Guild was one of the earliest in Reading, first mentioned in 1242.

All trace of any medieval building on the site of RISC has long since been obliterated, but it is probable that these plots, at the Kennet end of the street, were amongst the first to be built upon.

A lane apparently existed in 1552 to the north of no. 33, and the existence of alleys between 39-41 (now Sim's

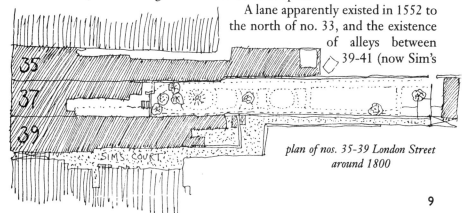

plan of nos. 35-39 London Street around 1800

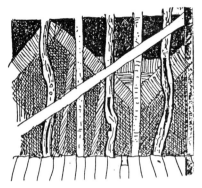

Court), and between 33 and the rear of modern no. 35 suggests early commercial use of the yards or gardens behind these houses, and also that they were substantial. Corner sites enjoyed more light; always a premium in a busy street, giving extra space here for busy traders. There is some timber framing on the interior walls of no. 37, and on the exterior wall of no. 39, which was very probably re-used from medieval structures on these sites. Its very durability suggests high quality, likely to have first been used in buildings of some importance.

The first documentary evidence for our three buildings comes in 1552, when Roger Amyce's great Survey of Reading records few vacant plots left in the street; the impression is one of a more or less continuous row of dwellings that were often quite substantial.

The Survey, of course, does not give house-numbers; but by matching entries with such other information as is available, Leslie Harman, the scrupulous historian of St Giles parish, felt confident enough to attach names to most properties.

According to Harman, the site of nos. 33-35 was then owned by John Leche, a dyer, and occupied by Simon Drewe; both served as street wardens and burghers. This was a substantial house, assessed at two shillings, the same amount as the house of Thomas Aldworth, a clothier and at one point Mayor of Reading, a few doors north of the RISC site. Numbers 37 and 39 were both owned by William Gray, and occupied respectively by William Benwell and Robert Adams, a Churchwarden in the 1530s.

No further information is available for Leche, but wills, both dated 1588, exist for one Bartholomew Benwell, a tailor of St Giles, and for Richard Adams. They may well have been relatives, perhaps sons, and the houses they describe are both substantial enough to have been found in London Street; but whether they really represent buildings on the site of RISC is any body's guess.

Assuming that they do, Benwell the tailor's house, on the site of no. 37, comprised a shop (containing board, shelves, shears), a hall, a buttery (where butts of ale or wine were stored), a kitchen, a chamber next to the street, a chamber over the entry, and a chamber over the hall.

The hall, and the chamber over it, had glass in the

windows – a sign of some wealth at this period. No glass at all is mentioned in Reading wills before 1570, and only occurs in 18% of Reading wills during the 1580s. Most people had to make do with shutters: the word 'window' is said to derive from 'wind eye' – you shut the shutters on the windy side. Glass windows were detachable and were often bequeathed. It was not unknown to take your windows with you when you moved.

Adams' house, on the site of 39, was even bigger. It contained eight rooms, placing it amongst the wealthiest 20% of contemporary Reading dwellings, and consisted of a shop, hall, cheese loft, milkhouse, inner chamber, 'next chamber', 'third chamber', a kitchen and a buttery. He kept pigs and had corn in store.

These houses could have been two or even three storeys high and maybe jettied; possibly with a frontage decorated with carved or moulded work on doorways and windows. The porch entry ascribed to no. 37 suggests stylish planning, and some degree of wealth; but it must be emphasised that there is no proof possible that the houses of the inventories were those on these sites – and that in any case none of the present structure is this old.

William Gray, the owner of nos. 37 and 39, was a courtier, a well-known versifier and song-writer. A favourite of Henry VIII, he was rewarded for his support of Henry VIII's 'policy' towards the Catholic Church – he abolished it, dissolving all abbeys, monasteries and religious bodies of every kind, and confiscating their property – with a huge grant of land and property in Reading that had formerly belonged to Reading Abbey. This may have had something to do with the Corporation's decision to choose him to serve as Reading's MP in 1547.

But fortunes change, and so do kings, and after Henry died Gray's faction at Court fell out of favour. Gray would almost certainly have been beheaded with the rest had he not had the presence of mind to die just in time. The Crown thus lost the chance to repossess his estates, and his widow inherited the lot. She remarried (for the fourth time) one John Blagrave, a cloth merchant, thereby ensuring the prosperity of the Blagrave family for centuries.

Gray is believed to have paid for stone and various architectural features that were removed from Reading Abbey, which brings us to an exciting discovery made during the restoration of the building by RISC: a host of carved stones from the Abbey, built into the basement of no. 35 and the wall between numbers 35 and 37.

Dr Ron Baxter of the Courtauld Institute of Art came to look at them. He is an expert on the stones of Reading Abbey, and has kindly allowed us to quote some extracts from a longer work he is producing:

Reading Abbey was built by King Henry I as his family mausoleum. When it was completed it was one of the four or five longest churches in the country. The elaborate arrangement of eastern chapels was paralleled in only two earlier English great churches, Bury St Edmund's and Anselm's 'glorious choir' at Canterbury of 1096, both renowned pilgrimage churches.

The stone used for the facing of the church came from the Taynton quarries in the Windrush valley, while for the elaborately-carved cloister, stone from Caen was shipped across the channel. The two stones are similar: both are fine-grained limestones, but Taynton stone is less regular, with distinctive shelly bands.

Although large parts of the monastic buildings survive, nothing of the church stands today except part of the south transept, stripped of its ashlar facing, a few choir-pier bases, and mounds of rubble marking the angles of the other transept. Even antiquarian drawings show us little more of its original appearance because demolition began early after the Dissolution and was unusually fast and thorough, owing largely to the convenience of having a source from which stone could be quarried in the centre of a thriving town.

The Abbey became Crown property after the Dissolution, and stood empty for nearly a decade. Then, in 1548, an estimate of the volume of lead on the roof was made, prior to its removal. From the following year we have a set of accounts kept by George Hynde, an official from the Court of Augmentations, recording receipts of money from people buying pieces of the Abbey fabric, payments to carpenters and labourers who worked in the demolition, and expenditure for materials like ropes and crowbars.

This document describes a rapid, almost wholesale demolition of the Abbey which must have transformed it almost beyond recognition. The beautifully carved cloister was sold off in two lots: Mr John Sands paid 50s for 'certen stones fallen downe upon two sydes of the Cloyster', and Mayster Greye 40s 'for the stone upon two sydes of the Cloyster'. Of John Sands nothing more is known, but it is thought that Mayster Greye was William Gray, the balladeer.

Gray also bought 'xv Jakes stoles', some plaster of Paris from the choir walls, the 'lytle rofe standing at the end of the Fratrye', 'a shedde and a wyndowe' and 'certayne stone that wente about the southe syde of the

Churche under Bartlements'. Some of the items are obviously functional (the Jakes [lavatory] stools and the shed), but others suggest an antiquarian or at least an aesthetic interest in the Abbey fabric. Apart from the cloister, which was richly carved, the window was presumably bought for its tracery, and the stone from under the battlements may have been a carved corbel table. This was not Grey's only venture into collecting. He also bought various items from St Lawrence's Church, Reading: the altar from the Chapel of St John, the Trinity Altar, and the cope chest.

At about this time three major building projects benefited from the availability of the Abbey fabric. Between 1550 and 1553 the Parish Church of St Mary's was rebuilt, using stone, timber and lead from the Abbey. In 1557, Abbey stone was used in the construction of the Poor Knight's Lodging at Windsor Castle. Then in 1562, 200 loads of stone from the Abbey were used for the repair of nineteen ruinous bridges in the Borough. Some of this repair work has recently been discovered in the covering of the Holy Brook.

In 1643 Reading was the site of a siege in the Civil War which had further serious effects on the Abbey. Defensive works were raised, running across the cloister from south to north, terminating in a hornwork which occupied a large part of the nave of the church. Stone for the construction of the rampart came, of course, from the Abbey, and further damage was caused during the ten days of bombardment necessary to obtain the surrender of the town.

In 1831 a building scheme was proposed which would have destroyed the ruins completely. This involved using the materials of the Abbey for road-building. The scheme was rejected by the town council, but this did not put an end to the destruction because the construction of both the 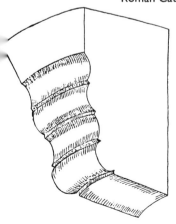 Roman Catholic church of St James (opened in 1840) and the new County Gaol (in 1843) involved demolition of parts of the Abbey fabric.

The quarrying of the Abbey since the reformation has taken stones to numerous sites within Reading and nearby.

Two celebrated discoveries of Reading material have been made this century: fifteen capitals and two voussoirs from Holme Park, Sonning (now Reading Blue Coat School), and some sixty carved stones used in the sixteenth century to shore up the river-bank at Borough Marsh, some two miles down the Thames. These last included two of the four great corner springers which marked the angles of the cloister arcade. These were easily the most massive of all the carved stones which made up the cloister arcade, requiring the strength of five men to remove them from the base of the wall where they were set.

Investigating Reading Abbey is like trying to complete an enormous three-dimensional jigsaw puzzle. The original box was lost long ago, and we have only a vague idea of what the completed picture should be. Furthermore, most of the pieces are lost too, and not only do we not know what they looked like, we do not even have any clear idea of how many there should be. As more pieces are found, the puzzle seems to get harder rather than easier, and this is true of the recent discoveries at 35 London Street, which do not obviously fit in with any of the other pieces on the tray. Nevertheless it seems certain that they are part of the same puzzle, if only because they are made of the right kind of stone: the limestone from which they are carved shows the shelly bands characteristic of the Taynton quarries.

Fragments of sculpture were discovered built into the fabric of no. 35 London Street during a major restoration of the building in 1997. The stones were found in two locations: (i) built into a wall on the first floor and (ii) built into walls in the basement. These walls must date from the period when the Abbey was in use as a quarry, most probably the late sixteenth or early seventeenth century. Two kinds of carved stone were found: voussoirs and scallop capitals. Voussoirs are the wedge-shaped stones used to form a semi-circular arch. Capitals are the carved stones which rest on top of a pier or column to support the arches above.

The voussoirs are carved with roll, and hollow mouldings, and there are three different profiles, or sections. I was able to examine seventeen of these voussoirs. Seven had been removed from the wall and their profiles could therefore be identified with certainty. The others were still in the wall, and it was sometimes impossible to tell which of the three profiles they had. This is not particularly crucial at this stage; what is more interesting is that the arches they originally formed were decorated with a multiplicity of simple mouldings.

Towards the end of the twelfth century, around 1170-1200, a new aesthetic of clean lines was beginning to replace the old preference for fussy complexity, and the first signs were the abandonment of intricate ornaments like chevron and billet in favour of multiple mouldings. Scallop capitals, on the other hand, first appear in the first years of the twelfth century at sites as far apart as Durham, Peterborough and the Tower of London. The scallop capital is simple in its basic design, but is capable of endless variation its details – all three of the London Street capitals are slightly different – and it was this capacity for variation which kept the design alive right to the end of the twelfth century.

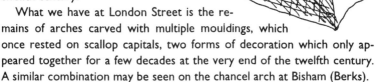

What we have at London Street is the remains of arches carved with multiple mouldings, which once rested on scallop capitals, two forms of decoration which only appeared together for a few decades at the very end of the twelfth century. A similar combination may be seen on the chancel arch at Bisham (Berks).

It is worth asking just what kind of structure within the Abbey the fragments originally came from. Both the capitals and the voussoirs are carved to suggest that they were originally engaged in a wall. Had they come from a free-standing structure like a cloister arcade they would have been carved on the back as well as the front. A doorway, window or wall arcade are the strongest candidates. The arch-span of only 1.27 metres would be uncomfortably narrow for a doorway. Another point to consider is that one of the capitals is carved on three of its faces – a feature normally found on only the most elaborate multiple portal arrangements, like the reconstructed west doorway at St Nicholas's, Abingdon. Turning to the voussoirs, their three different profiles could have come from a row of arches of different designs, or they could have been nested, one inside another, to form a deeply-recessed arch of several orders. Experience suggests that the second alternative is more likely: it is very unusual to find a row of arches with different moulded profiles. We must therefore conclude that the pieces probably came either from a wall-arcade or from the surrounds of a multiple window composition, although there is nothing to tell us whereabouts in the Abbey complex it might have been.

15

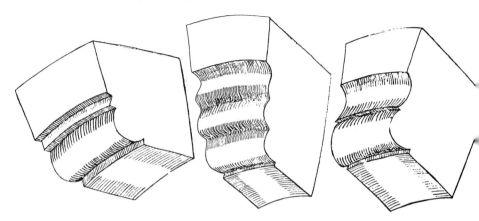

Finding the stones was one of the highlights of RISC's restoration programme. John Lloyd:

> The stones were first uncovered during the creation of a new doorway into the conference room. The carving on several of the stones was of considerable interest, so a decision was made to continue removing stones from the rest of the wall.
>
> During the next several days a large number of stones were removed. When the dreaded deadline for the plastering of the wall finally came, about half of them were found to be carved with a variety of mouldings or mason's marks. The collection contained examples of four distinct arch mouldings and three capitals, including sufficient stone for one complete arch. It is a pity that the project could not have continued indefinitely, as it seems likely that the stones to finish the job were right there, but there was still much work to be done to make the room usable and deadlines are an unhappy fact of life.
>
> At this point we had rather a large pile of interesting stones, and it was time to decide exactly what to do with them. Some ideas ('chuck 'em in the skip') were rejected outright; others, such as the plan to build them in over a doorway, were appealing but not practical given the dimensions of the room. The possibility of constructing a single nested arch was also tempting, but impractical given the room's

location on the first floor, as ensuring sufficient support would have been a major headache.

In the end a wall arcade was chosen as the best way to display the stones, consistent with structural stability and the basic proportions of the room. It was also preferable to keep as much of the installation as possible within two areas of old, soft brickwork, while retaining the central section of modern, hard brickwork to ensure adequate support for the roof.

The construction of the stones' new home started out with a series of chalk markings, taking the dimensions of the single complete arch as the pattern for the rest. Then bricks were cut away and replaced with stone. The stones were packed out with pieces of slate and tile, with the margins of the holes shaped to fit with a relatively soft mix of sand and cement. Lime mortar would have been preferable, but we didn't have the time to get some. Throughout the reconstruction we attempted to minimise contact between the stone and cement. Lime mortar was to be used at a later stage (when time was less pressing) to fill the joints between the stones.

During the installation of the stones time capsules containing the daily newspapers and RISC leaflets were sealed into the wall cavity. This should provide an established time frame and context for the work, and make life easier for future archaeologists.

Finding the stones prompted Pete Hay to a spot of sculptural eavesdropping:

I like the idea of buried treasure. The buzz of discovery. So on a first tour of the dark cellar, the Romanesque carved capital embedded in the wall seemed like some 'mysterious sympathy', a confirmation that this book would be a good thing to do. Then the hacking of plaster from the meeting room wall exposed more. Before the dust had settled, John and

17

> Martin extracted enough toothy voussoirs of the same moulding to create an arch, which John meticulously reconstructed. Thereby recycling and restituting the communal charitable spirit of the original, which is what this book is partly about. Stones have stories. Walls have ears. Dave gave me some tools and I made my Van Gogh offering to plug in as a stony metaphor for silence and a willingness to listen. The electronic bugging device is not connected. Yet.

In theory, the stones in no. 35-37 could have been removed at any time before the mid-nineteenth century, when Abbey-looting began to become slightly less acceptable, but it is at least intriguing that they make up a complete arch, for it strongly suggests that it was taken very early on, when there were still complete arches left to take.

Gray's penchant for the more attractive stones raises the interesting possibility that the arch may have been selected for the Versifier himself, and subsequently given (or sold) by Gray or his heirs to his tenant at No. 37 for building materials. (Thomas Aldworth, whom the 1552 survey suggests was in the process of buying, perhaps building himself a substantial mansion in London Street at this time, also bought a lot of Abbey stone). Maybe they were even reconstructed to become a feature – a window, perhaps? – before the house was rebuilt and the stones built into the wall. This is all surmise, of course, but it does seem likely that the stones have been on this site since the mid-sixteenth century, implying a major rebuild at that time.

Although no structural evidence survives for a building at no. 35 above ground level, the cellar below the present house is intriguing, for the vaulting of the cellar roof appears to have originally continued under the alley-way. A possible first use for the stone now in the cel-lar might therefore have been to con-struct it in the six-teenth century.

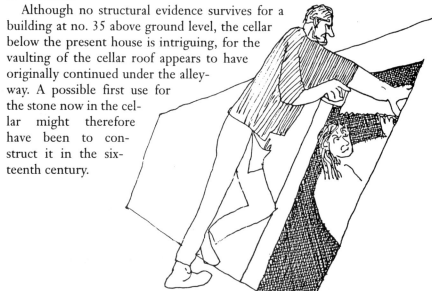

2: of friends and beer

Antipathy to state religion was a feature of Reading, as with many towns dominated by large religious institutions. In 1498 four traders of Lollard sympathies were punished for entertaining 'certayn mystering and evil techying personnes', but few then could have guessed that the mighty Abbey itself would disappear within a generation.

The townsfolk fell with alacrity to the work of removing the tangible traces of the Catholic church. In 1549, the Fair Cross in London Street was smashed; and Protestant ways of thinking spread swiftly amongst the town's leading citizens. The first will to include a 'Protestant' commendation of a Reading citizen's soul to the afterworld occurs in 1554, and by the 1570s only one testator out of thirty-four was using 'Catholic' wording.

Protestant feeling, or more correctly anti-Catholic feeling, continued to grow in the town. There was uproar when the ambassador of the arch-Catholic King of Spain passed through Reading in 1623, and a decade later one Ludowick Bowyer was branded on both cheeks for spreading rumours that Archbishop Laud was in league with the Pope. Laud, the most reactionary prelate since the Reformation, was ironically a Reading lad, the son of a Broad Street mercer. He was appointed by Stuart monarchs to restore the Church hierarchy and with it the Divine Right of Kings. It made him extremely unpopular, in Reading and elsewhere. His attempt to impose his own nominee as an MP for the town was indignantly rejected, and when he was beheaded in 1645 his body was paraded through the streets.

By now the Civil War had broken out, and the town suffered mightily, 'possibly more so than any other English town', according to Professor Slade: it was taken and re-taken five times. In 1649 Charles II was beheaded, and Cromwell assumed power as 'Lord Protector'; and for a few brief years people were allowed to practice whatever religious beliefs they chose to. Geoff Sawers picks up the thread:

> In the turbulent years of the 1650s the collapse of the King's control over the church allowed numerous and diverse religious groups to flourish, and freedom of the press under the Commonwealth meant that anyone could publish their ideas.
>
> A prominent group to develop at this time was George Fox's Society of Friends, who denied dogma and legalism, accepting only the guidance of the 'inner light' of God inside. They were known, derisively, as 'Quakers', and once the monarchy was restored in 1660 they were persecuted relentlessly. But their ideas had spread too widely and taken too good a root to be easily quashed.
>
> Reading was a strong centre for all kinds of nonconformity and when Fox first came here in 1655, staying with his old friend Thomas Curtis, a wealthy woollen-draper, he found a large audience. The Reading Quakers were, throughout the 1660s, to fill Reading Gaol with such regularity but with such obvious disinclination to recant and such belief in their eventual vindication that the Justices were brought occasionally to despair. The authorities were dumbfounded when, with all the adult Quakers in gaol, the meetings were continued by the children.
>
> Fox had been outraged at the (then not uncommon) idea that 'women have no souls, no more than a goose'. In the Quakers, women were equal with men. This caused much contention, particularly over the institution of separate women's meetings for their business (distribution of money to the poor, placing young women as maids etc.). In Reading, Thomas and Ann Curtis, who owned the meeting house in 'the Sun backside' (behind the 'Sun' pub in King Street) objected to the women's meetings. The differences became so heated that in 1684 the Curtises and their party locked the meeting house doors on those who supported the women,s meetings and moved to another room nearby.
>
> The others (the 'orthodox' meeting) went to meet in the cottage of a widow named Ann Truse for a few years and then in 1692 took on the rent of a larger house from a woman called Elizabeth Bryant. The Quarter Sessions licence for this building describes it as being 'in the Court or backside behind a Messuage or Tenement on the East side of London Street'. This, by reliable tradition, was held to be Sims' Court, behind no. 39 London Street.
>
> The dispute over the women's meetings is indicative of what seems a very distinct divide between the two groups. The Curtises' party was richer, but also contained more dependent poor which might account for a greater class-consciousness among them. Their minutes for instance never

record the first names of poor members, but say 'paid Scotford for sweeping' or 'the woman Mosdell...' By contrast, in the Orthodox meeting's minutes, even if a person's first name is unknown a space is left for it to be filled in later. It was to this 'Orthodox' meeting that the great Quaker leader William Penn (who had published a defence of women's meetings) would come on his visits to Reading.

Penn was born in October 1644, at the time of the second Battle of Newbury. Entering Oxford at the age of 16, young Penn was a good-looking and popular boy, and a notable athlete, but his rejection of the formalist theology of the day soon caused him problems. 'I never had any religion other than what I felt', he would write later, and further 'I never addicted myself to school learning to understand religion by, but always, even to their faces, rejected and disputed against it'. He was sent down from Oxford for his nonconformity after just a year. He was something of a gallant, at least enough to inspire a twinge of jealousy in Samuel Pepys when he came home one day in 1663 to find the fashionably-dressed Penn there talking to his wife.

WILLIAM PENN.

From a small ivory model in basso relievo by Silvanus Bevan a contemporary of William Penn, in the possession of Paul Bevan near London. The original from which the portraits of William Penn have been taken.

Pepys probably need not have worried; Penn was already leaning towards Quakerism and in 1667, at a meeting in Ireland he was convinced. Quakers would not conduct their meetings in secret as other sects did, and within months Penn was up before the magistrate for his ejection of a soldier who was disrupting a meeting. The magistrate, surprised that a gentleman should be a Quaker, offered him a pardon but he refused the privilege of his rank and went to prison with his fellows.

Thus began a long career in which Penn was imprisoned often (to the dismay of his father, an Admiral) and released often but never ceased to write and worship how he would. He campaigned tirelessly for religious toleration, not just for Quakers but for all the sects even including the Catholics. (Fox had urged Cromwell to lead his armies to sack Rome!)

Penn's urbanity, as well as his commitment, allowed him to become toleration's most influential advocate at court. His defence of the generally unpopular Catholics helped him to maintain a friendship with the Duke of York (King Charles II's brother, Lord High Admiral and later James II), and in 1681 he obtained, in settlement for a debt of £16,000 from the Crown to his father, a grant of land in America about the size of England to the west of Delaware. This was to become Pennsylvania, his ideal community, where liberty of conscience was foremost. (Pennsylvania achieved an ironic fame with the nuclear accident at Three Mile Island in 1979; despite the proximity of AWE Burghfield and Aldermaston Reading has so far been spared this!). Unfortunately for Penn, those whom he left in charge of the colony in his absence (including his dissolute son, whom he had hoped would succeed him) did not share his ideals and concepts such as fair dealing with the native Americans were swiftly dropped.

Penn's second visit to the colony in 1699-1701 was a terrible shock, and within a few years, tricked out of his business interest there by his dishonest steward, he was almost bankrupted. He retired disillusioned to a house in Ruscombe, near Twyford, 'on a noble large dry gravely green, and clean ways about it...', and it was from here that he would, when well enough, ride in to Reading on a Sunday to attend the Quaker meeting.

A series of strokes in 1712 robbed him of the power of articulate speech and in his last years he delighted only in his garden and grandchildren; smiling at visitors and old friends but unable to say more than a few words.

One thing that must have cheered him in his dotage was that the two Quaker factions, both desiring new premises, managed to reunite in 1715 when they moved to their present site, just around the corner in Church Street.

('whereas we have made an offer of reconciliation...we desire yt all things relating to former differences to be laid aside...not to judge one another any more for not practicing things wherein we have not faith and condemning others for practicing what they believe is their duty...' Reply: 'We shall be well pleased to see you come and sit down with us').

Not that, even after the Toleration Act of 1690, renewed by Queen Anne in 1703, their sufferings were over. 'Persons of substance in the parish (St Giles) are few and thin and there's abundance of Quakers there who will not pay anything to the church rates', wailed one poor clerk in 1724; Quakers were still having their possessions impounded for non-payment of these rates well into the next century.

Penn died at Ruscombe on 30 July 1718 and was buried not in Reading but at Chalfont St Giles in Buckinghamshire. A young Reading Quaker named Edward Behon recorded in his diary that a number of Reading Friends accompanied the corpse, and that the next morning 'a dreadful tempest of thunder' set barns on fire and destryed crops around. Penn's passing clearly needed to be marked.

Though to Penn himself, his ideals and ambitions might have seemed to have been eclipsed, his example was an inspiration to many, and place him firmly in the same tradition as George Lovejoy and RISC itself. His house in Reading was eventually demolished in 1840, to make way for the railway. Eliza Langley, a fellow Quaker who took over Lovejoy's library on his death, commissioned a plaque to Penn's memory in 1886. It was erected in the Bookshop at no. 39, where it stayed until the great fire of 1973. The plaque was rescued from the wreckage by David Hutchings, and was eventually donated to Blake's Lock Museum, where it is still on display.

Reading's famous cloth industry, which in the sixteenth century had employed well over a third of the working population, declined rapidly in the next century in the face of competition from other parts of the country. By 1681 the number of clothiers had dropped from 160 to 12, and the decline brought with it a great deal of poverty. Occupants for grand houses in places such as London Street became harder to find, and in 1638 the Corporation tried to prevent 'covetous persons' who 'daily more and more subdivide divers messuages and larger houses, fairly built and fit for the dwellings of men of better fortune, into small dwellings, or rather into obscure receptacles of poor people'.

It is probably at this date that the first 'slum' cottages were built in Sims' Court; and there is some evidence to suggest that the houses at nos. 37 and 39 were rebuilt at this time.

The fire of 1973 revealed that the party wall between the two houses had been supported by an oak tree of seventeenth-century date, which by now had rotted away and had to be replaced. The footings in no. 39 had to be underpinned, and the builders found chalk and flint rubble, which an expert from the University thought also dated from the seventeenth century: the flint might have come from the Abbey, still Reading's favourite quarry.

Beer proved to be Reading's salvation. Demand for beer increased steadily throughout the century – in 1684 excise duty was paid on 6,318,000 barrels, which works out at almost forty gallons for every man, woman and child, and a good deal more was brewed privately. London, which was growing rapidly, was particularly thirsty; and Reading, at the heart of a major barley-growing area, with good road and water connections with the capital, flourished accordingly. In the 1740s-60s, enough malt was exported from Berkshire to London each year to produce 400,000 barrels of medium-strength beer; and by 1760 it had become the most important malting area in Britain.

'Very great quantities of malt, and meal' were sent to London by barge, according to Daniel Defoe; and London Street's proximity to the Kennet and its wharves, not to mention St Giles Mill in Mill Lane, once more put the street at the centre of the town's trade. As late as 1807 a house close to nos. 35-39, formerly the home of a bargemaster, was described as 'in London Street' but 'facing' Boults' Wharf.

Malthouses and granaries appeared on the land behind the houses, which were increasingly occupied by malsters, meal-men and bargemasters. The street was once more prosperous, perhaps the most prosperous street in town, and a lot of fine fancy facades were added to older, timber-framed buildings.

Parish poor-rate books survive from 1745, and from now it becomes possible to reconstruct the pattern of occupation and usage of nos. 35-39 with a fair degree of accuracy.

The house at no. 35 was assessed in 1750 at 14s 7.5d, when it was oc-cupied by William Edmunds and from 1757 by one John Barnard, an Overseer of the Poor. In 1772 Thomas Saunders took it over, and its val-ue jumps from £16 (in 1766) to £22; which suggests some major structur-al improvements at that date, if not a complete rebuild. There is some structural evidence to support this, for in the cellar the external wall shows evidence of windows which match a Georgian fenestration, but does not accord with the later baroque frontage.

Six years later the occupant was Robert Harris, later his widow Mrs Harris, who continued to pay the rates until 1820. Harris was both a ben-eficiary and a trustee of Thomas Saunders' own will, which was so com-plicated that they had to resort to a private Act of Parliament in 1813 to sort it out; it seems probable that Harris was actually holding this proper-ty in trust for Saunders' heirs.

No. 33 was built on the front of a much larger plot that appears to have belonged to no. 35. The substantial area of land behind the house con-tained a fair-sized malthouse, occupied in 1745 by James Buy or Bye, in 1749 described as a 'meal man' who had other properties elsewhere. A stable was added to the rate assessment from 1768, and a granary in 1772. Saunders paid the rates on the malthouse in 1774, and was further as-sessed for a 'chaise-house' (the post-chaise was the fashionable way to travel long distances in the late eighteenth century), but the next year, when the house itself was let to a gentleman, the Rev Mr Weighnhouse, the malthouse reverted to Buy.

In 1778 the malthouse passed to Robert Harris junior. This is probably the same Robert Harris who in 1790 co-founded the Reading 'coun-try' bank of Stephens, Harris and Stephenson. He became Mayor in 1818 and died in 1840, 'an old and highly re-spected inhabitant', according to the Chronicle.

In 1797, for that year only, rates for the Harris malt-house were charged to William Blackall Simonds, new-ly installed at his Seven Bridges Brewery and clearly in need of extra supplies or storage to service his rapidly-ex-panding business. Simonds', later Courage's, Reading brewery eventually became one of the largest and

most famous in the land, and was not demolished until the 1980s: the giant Oracle development is about to be built on the site.

Number 37 was in 1750 occupied by Thomas Edmunds, who was assessed at the same figure, 14s 7.5d, as William Edmunds (presumably related) next door at no. 35; but by 1766 the house was valued at only £12, £4 less than no. 35, suggesting that the building had become considerably run down.

In 1780 the house had a new occupant, Charles Toovey, and was valued at £20. A major improvement is indicated, perhaps a complete rebuild: the 'A' frame roof, pegged and without a ridge pole, is eighteenth-century, and contemporary internal alterations include sash windows, mezzanine floors, additional front and back staircases connecting extra floors, taller rooms with taller windows, and the extensive attic areas with dormer windows behind the parapet. It was a respectable Georgian town house, in short: an acceptable address for an attorney such as John Biggs, who moved there in 1805.

a mansarded roof

The earliest clear reference to Number 39 in the rate-books occurs in 1781, and it is possible that this house was rebuilt at that date, perhaps in conjunction with no. 37 which it closely resembles. The party-wall chimney is probably eighteenth century, and a sawn-off great beam in the attic suggests that the two roofs may once have been combined.

Although this house is slightly larger, the rateable value was consistently lower. This may be because the building behind the house apparently belonged to no. 37 – an anomaly perhaps best explained by a common owner for both properties at one point. In 1780/81 the rates for no. 39 were paid by John Hewell Hill, who might have been the builder of both houses. (The building in the yard was in 1814 described as a granary, and in that year was let to Daniel Jones, a well-known London Street saddlemaker. It seems possible that it forms the nucleus of the present extension behind no. 39: although the curious mansarded roof was added later in the nineteenth century, the walls are much thicker than would be expected for a structure of this date.)

The owner in 1782 was Joseph Morris, a prosperous Minster Street grocer and Quaker, who apparently settled the property on his daughter Elizabeth: she paid the rates in December 1787. The fol-

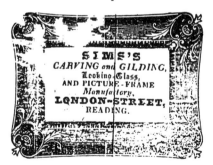

advert in Reading Mercury *1825*

lowing March she married Thomas Speakeman. The house may have been part of her dowry, for thereafter the assessment is in his name. He also paid for a granary and warehouse, presumably behind the house and approached through Sims' Court. From 1796 the house was occupied by Charles Baker, whose family remained there until 1816. A succession of occupants followed until 1827, when Mrs Tull of Streatley moved in; and

stairwell at no. 35

in 1838 she sold the property to George Lovejoy – about whom much more anon.

The ownership of nos. 39 and 41 in 1807 passed to George Sims, a carpenter, together with three, later four houses in Sims' Court behind the houses. These were small cottages, in 1846 valued at only £4 each (no. 37, by comparison, was worth £35), and in that year all the occupants were assessed as 'poor'. Some of the cottages survived until 1958 when David Hutchings joined the Bookshop: 'There was a water-pump by the cottages, and an old unused gaslight.'

There's some evidence to suggest that the Quakers had used Sims' Court as a route to their burying-ground in modern Sidmouth Street, and one thing to emerge clearly from our exciting study of the rate-books is a strong and enduring connection between our three houses and the Quakers. James Buy and Joseph Morris were certainly Friends, and Thomas Speakeman married Morris' daughter. Thomas Saunders in 1785 witnessed the will of another Quaker neighbour; Robert Harris was a close friend of his, quite literally a trustee. (Sims was the odd one out, though a nonconformist too: a prominent Unitarian. His sect met at his own workshops in Mill Lane until 1813, when they moved into an old Baptist chapel in London Street.)

Such an unusual concentration around the former 'Orthodox' chapel suggests that the seventeenth-century occupants of the houses on our site may all have been members of the breakaway group. It also explains how the existence of the chapel was remembered – and its connection with William Penn, the most famous Quaker of them all.

The malt trade went into decline in the early nineteenth century, and the malthouses and granaries of London Street began, slowly, to disappear. But once more London Street swiftly found a new vocation, this time as a centre for the booming coaching trade. A coach-building manufactory opened close to the High Bridge, and in 1822 Joseph Huntley, a Quaker, opened a small bakery opposite the Crown Inn, where he made biscuits that sold well to coach travellers. (He later went into partnership with a Mr Palmer. 'They did all right', as James Matthews said.)

Saddlers and harness-makers set up shop in the street, and the granaries were converted into stable-blocks; but the focus of the street's coaching connection was the new Post Office which Charles Skeate White, the town's Postmaster, opened at no. 37 in 1811.

The Post Office was an important place, for it was here that news from the outside world first reached Reading. The British victory at Waterloo in 1814 was publicly announced from the steps of no. 37 by Mr Moody, proprietor of the one o'clock coach from London, who had presumably rushed – 'post-haste', indeed – down from the capital with the news. A letter from a Reading man, containing an eye-witness account of the battle, was later read aloud from the same place 'and those assembled to hear it gave three ringing cheers for the British Army'.

Richard Sims, gilder and carver and presumably a relation of George Sims the carpenter, painted several 'transparencies' for the occasion. Napoleon's carriage, complete with coachman, had been captured at the battle and made a brief appearance in Reading: it was paraded down London Street on its way to public exhibition in the Forbury. In July, a Peace Feast was held in London Street. Tables were set up along the whole length of the street, and 6,000 people sat down to dine at the Corporation's expense.

London Street had been busy during the Napoleonic War. 'The drum and fife and the trumpet call of the Blues were constantly heard in London Street', a former resident recalled. 'One day about the year 1813 I saw a long line of French prisoners escorted down London Street...who presented a very miserable appearance.' Five of the street's pubs were used as headquarters for the 'recruiting parties' of soldiers who scoured the streets for hapless young men, dragged into the Army with a 'King's Shilling' thrust deftly into their hands by unscrupulous recruiting sergeants.

3:of books and peace

At some time before 1817, Mrs Harris (probably the widow of Robert Harris senior) one Robinson opened a book shop in a single-story annexe on the south side of her house at no. 33. In that year his business was taken over by Edmund Havell, bookseller, stationer and drawing master and a member of a well-known family of Reading artists, who augmented his stock with 'every possible variety of Colours, Brushes, Papers, Portfolios and other Articles required in Drawing'. He soon set up a Circulating Library, with a surprising sideline as grocer and tea-dealer. Tea was still a high-class product then; although, as a Reading man observed in 1815, it was already becoming something 'which a modern Englishman cannot do without'. Today, fair-traded beverages still share space with books. Edmund's progeny, his grandson, Ernest Binfield Havell was another pioneer of international solidarity, helping to revive an indigenous school of Indian painting in Madras and Calcutta. He was fervently involved in the resurgence of handloom weaving, famously blessed

L. HAVELL,

NEAR THE BRIDGE, LONDON-STREET,

READING,

BEGS leave to inform his Friends and the Public he has opened a SHOP in the OIL and COLOUR line. He flatters himself the knowledge he has of preparing Colours for use, will recommend him to the notice of those who wish to do their own Painting.

Greens for Fencing, mixed to any Pattern.
White Lead, Dry or Ground.
Chocolate, Lead Colour, Tar Brown, &c.
Fine Florence Oil, Anchovies, and every Article in the Oil Trade.

☞ PAINTING and GLAZING in the neatest manner, as usual.

Luke Havell was Edmund's father

by Gandhi. As the somewhat critical *Times* obituary of 1935 stated: 'The traditional art of India...was not dead, but merely sleeping or smothered by the blanket of European culture laid upon it for a century and a half. It needed only to be released from this incubus to regain its pristine vigour'.

In 1832, Havell sold his premises to William Stubbs Fynmore, who moved into the house at no. 35 with his family. The book shop was taken over by George Lovejoy; Fynmore, in partnership with John Jenner, traded from the shop next door as tea-dealers and oilmen.

In 1842, no. 35 was substantially rebuilt. The Mechanics Institute was then being constructed next door, and Fynmore & Jenner added the present grand baroque frontage to their property. It was built of the Bath stone that was becoming very popular, and its scale and splendour stand up well to the porticoed front of the Institute, still London Street's most imposing building.

Other alterations to no. 35 may date from this time. The building has a splendid staircase and a very fine front-door with an inset glass coach-

lamp above. The cellar, now a kitchen, was also extended around this date. Three large barrel-vaults were built under the pavement; and the kitchen stoves, slate flooring and a small half-barrel vault are all nineteenth century too.

The cellar had a window, now covered in but still discernible. In 1810, *The Stranger in Reading*, a wonderfully barbed guide to the town's shortcomings, complained about the state of the pavements in London Street, and singled out 'a cellar window, wide open, and extending nearly across the footpath'. *The Stranger*'s observations spurred a complacent Corporation into action, and in 1813 the street was re-paved. The gradient of the street was altered slightly, with spoil from the upper part used to raise the lower part. This explains why houses at the top of the street now have several front-doorsteps – and why so many cellar windows, like that at no. 35, have disappeared.

In 1838, the celebrated George Lovejoy moved into Mrs Tull's old

house at no. 39. It soon became one of Reading's most famous landmarks, and an essential rendezvous for 'the carriage people'. Alan Hankin, local studies librarian at Reading Library, takes up the tale:

George Lovejoy was a Reading man through and through. Born in St Mary's parish, he was educated in St Laurence's, and made his name in St Giles'. His part in this story concerns his Circulating Library, Post Office receiving house, Stationers, Publishers, and Printers at 39 London Street, but first a little background.

He was born on 8 February 1808 in Earley Court, a cluster of cottages reached from Earley Place, off Minster Street. The cottages are long gone, and the whole area is due to be comprehensively transformed by the Oracle shopping centre, but Earley Place may well be familiar to readers who have collected items from Heelas.

His education was unremarkable. As an infant he attended a 'Dame School' run by a Mrs Slyfield before going, at around eight years old, to the National School in the Abbey Ruins. This had been founded in 1813 and was situated in the Chapter House, where two rooms were built, big enough, it was claimed, for 300-400 children, and apartments provided for the Master and Mistress.

At the age of 14, in 1822, Lovejoy left school and started work. He tried his hand at a couple of jobs (including working for a grocer called Wicks) before becoming apprenticed as a bookseller and printer, to Messrs Smart and Cowslade, publishers of the *Reading Mercury*: the first, and at the time the only, Reading newspaper. Their printing works were in Market Place 'at the sign of the Bible and Crown'. His job included travelling outside

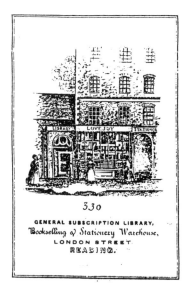

330

GENERAL SUBSCRIPTION LIBRARY,
Bookselling & Stationery Warehouse,
LONDON STREET
READING.

Reading, and in March 1829 an attachment developed between George and Martha Wilkinson, a young lady a few years older than him (she was born in April 1803, so was 25 at this point while George was 21). On a Sunday in May 1830 they went on a trip to Windsor and Eton, where, like countless star-crossed lovers before and since, they carved their initials in a tree.

George Lovejoy

Having worked for the Cowslades for 10 years, the question arose of George setting up shop separately. He went to Odiham with Darter to look at a site, but eventually agreed terms with Mr Fynmore to take over Havell's shop and warehouse, which one of his old workers, quoted in *In Memoriam George Lovejoy* and looking back to 50 years before, recalls as being 'next door to what was then Champion's granary and corn stores, and a tumble-down old building used as a cooperage.'

GEORGE LOVEJOY SUCCESSOR TO MR. EDMUND HAVELL, *STATIONER, BOOKBINDER, BOOKSELLER* and *ENGRAVER* 120, LONDON-STREET, READING NEXT THE POST OFFICE *Respectfully informs the inhabitants of Reading and Neighbourhood that he has taken the shop occupied by MR. EDMUND HAVELL, and has now on sale every kind of* plain and *fancy stationery to which he earnestly solicits their* attention, assuring them all *diligence* shall be used to merit their kind support. All *genuine Patent Medicines* and Perfumery New Works and *Periodicals* on the day of *Publication.* CIRCULATING LIBRARY *(Reading Mercury, 3 September 1832)*

Monday 3 September 1832 was opening day, and the first income was half-a-crown from a Miss Green of Wargrave. Quite what she bought is not recorded, but let us hope she enjoyed it.

He was by no means independent of the Cowslades and continued to work for them as well as running his. He was also doing other things, start-

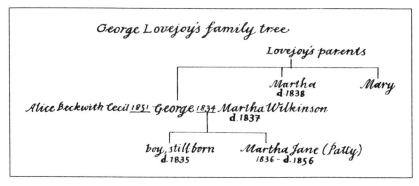

George Lovejoy's family tree

Lovejoy's parents

Martha
d.1838

Mary

Alice Beckwith Cecil 1851 — George 1834 Martha Wilkinson
d.1837

boy, still born
d.1835

Martha Jane (Patty)
1836 - d.1856

ing a book club and becoming an agent for Globe Insurance, and in December 1832 took on a public duty by being sworn in as a sheriff's deputy.

1834 was a momentous year for George Lovejoy. Francis Cowslade died, which prompted his brother Frederick ('Mr Fred' to George) to re-align his company. In future they would concentrate on newspaper production, so their own business had to be off-loaded. Lovejoy had first option, and took it.

On 16 September came the culmination of 5 years' courtship. George Lovejoy and Martha Wilkinson were married at St Leonard's Church, Wallingford.

They had two children, but, tragically, the first, a boy, was still-born. On 2 June 1836 was born their daughter, christened Martha Jane but known to family and friends as Patty. She was the apple of her father's eye. One year later, Patty was without a mother, Martha having contracted consumption (better known now as TB, and increasing in prevalence again). She died on 25 November 1837 and is buried at St Giles. George Lovejoy knew his share of family tragedies. His younger sister Mary, who never married, moved in with him to run the house and look after Patty. The other sister, Martha, Mrs Champ, died in 1838. At the time of the 1841 census, the household of George and Mary Lovejoy included Elizabeth Champ, probably their niece.

After his first wife's death George Lovejoy remained a single parent, aided by his sister. He eventually did marry again, but not for 14 years, when his bride was Alice Beckwith Cecil, daughter of an Oxford solicitor. They were wed at All Saints, Oxford, on 11 January 1851. Mary Lovejoy stayed with them for a while, but by 1861 she had moved next door to number 37, the old Post Office.

In the meantime George experienced yet another bereavement:

DEATHS On the 4th inst., in London-street, Reading, in her 21st year, Martha Jane, the beloved daughter of Mr. George Lovejoy, bookseller. (*Reading Mercury*, 6 September 1856)

George Lovejoy properly enters this story in July 1838, when he moved into no. 39. It was then a private house, most recently inhabited by Mrs Tull, who had died in April. (She was 'relict of John Tull, of Southridge, Berks', Southridge being in Streatley, where it is the name of a farm.) He kept up both sites for a while (the Directories of Reading for 1839 and 1841 record 'Mr Lovejoy' at this address, but still show the Library and bookshop at no. 33), but when the Fynmore property was demolished in 1842 to make way for the Mechanics Institute, Lovejoy moved his business to no. 39. On the larger premises the business could expand. The building behind the shop, fronting onto Sims Court and believed to be on the site of the Quaker meeting house, was rebuilt or substantially converted, and housed Lovejoy's celebrated Circulating Library.

This was the most famous of Lovejoy's many activities, but in the early years he faced competition from a number of other booksellers, principally John Snare of Minster Street and Messrs Rusher & Johnson of King Street, but George Lovejoy was the younger man and took on these older firms by taking advantage of cheaper publications and setting out more attractive window displays. It was recalled on his death that the Circulating Library was at its peak in the 40s and 50s, but it was also remembered as the largest circulating library in the South, if not anywhere in the kingdom outside London, with 70,000-80,000 volumes. One business card calls the establishment 'The British & Foreign Library — by Special Appointment to Her Majesty'.

George Lovejoy had definite ideas on the sorts of books he should stock:

25-27-29-31 **Long, Son & Everard,** general drapers and silk mercers · 'Phone No. 46
25 Long, Walter H.
  Primitive Methodist Chapel

33-35 HEDLEY BROWN, Bookbinder, Printer, Picture Framer and Artists' Colourman

Dann & Lewis, Photographers
Lewis, Henry, dissolving view artist
Johnson Bros., Ltd., dyers
39 **Long, William C.,** Bookseller, stationer, and librarian ; house and estate agent ; life and fire insurance agent
41 **Deed, Arthur, Chemist and** photographic material dealer
43 Ward, Lorraine, photographer
45 Swaite, Frederick J., grocer

from Yorke's Reading Street Key *1839*

LOVEJOY'S LIBRARY, BOOKSELLING AND GENER-
AL PAPER WAREHOUSE, LONDON-STREET, READ-
ING This large and long established Library contains
many Thousand Volumes in every department of
Literature, and whilst the prevailing popular taste of a
lighter class is adequately supplied, the Proprietor has
felt desirous to extensively add Works of a higher and
more enduring character. The encouragement received for the past
years pleasingly proves that the course pursued has met with the appro-
bation of an enlightened public. (*Reading Mercury* 28 September 1839)

Through the Southern Counties Library George Lovejoy established
friendships with some notable literary figures, chief amongst these Charles
Dickens. In 1841 he corresponded with Dickens about the possibility of
Dickens standing for Parliament (Lovejoy was prominent in local Liberal
politics, but never stood for election to the council). Mary Russell Mitford,
author of *Our Village*, received much of her reading material from George

Lovejoy, and his daughter 'Patty' became one of Miss Mitford's favourites.

The Library was an important meeting place. It was chosen to display a portrait of Queen Victoria after her accession:

We have just seen at Lovejoy's Library a PORTRAIT of HER MAJESTY by Mr DAWE, an artist of first rate talent. The PORTRAIT represents her Majesty in the dress she has appeared in at St George's Chapel and we consider it a most excellent likeness of our young and amiable Sovereign. (*Reading Mercury* 2 November 1839)

It was also the place to go for tickets to see Whiteknights, now, of course, the campus of the University of Reading, but at the time still recognisable as the wonderful landscaped garden created by the Marquess of Blandford, heir to the Dukedom of Marlborough:

This opportunity is taken of announcing that the SPLENDID GARDENS and GROUNDS at WHITE-KNIGHTS, late the seat of the Duke of Marlborough, so celebrated for his Horticultural Taste, will continue, for a time, open for inspection. Application for Admission tickets to be made to Mr. Lovejoy, Library, Reading. (*Reading Mercury* 28 September 1839)

As well as dealing in books, George Lovejoy was also a stationer, describing his wares in the following terms in 1838:

all kinds of WRITING PAPERS can be supplied at the Library, on the most advantageous terms; together with the best qualities of WAX, INK, PENS, PENCILS —— OUTSIDES and SCRIBBLING PAPER very cheap. (*Reading Mercury* 13 October 1838)

He also had the local dealership, for 'HURLEY and Co's highly-esteemed ENEKEMELAN, or DURABLE BLACK WRITING INK'. Amongst its various excellent qualities, the following are submitted as of the first importance, viz.:

It remains in a constant state of fluidity. It imparts (though pale on writing) a splendid and durable black:. It flows freely from and does not clog the pen, and Being (by a process in the manufacture hitherto unknown, including that of filtration) divested of mucilage, will not coagulate. One trial will prove this fact. (*Reading Mercury* 6 July 1835)

In later years he produced his own writing equipment, including 'Lovejoy's Self-Adapting Pen', which was, if his adverts are to be believed, very well received:

Having tried Mr Lovejoy's new self-adapting metallic pens, we must say that we prefer them to any of the other kinds of steel pens that we have hitherto written with; their extreme flexibility gives them a decided superiority over others, therefore we can take it on ourselves to recommend them strongly to all lovers of free and easy writing.
Guernsey Sun

Besides selling and lending books, George Lovejoy was a publisher and printer. In publishing, he was responsible for one of the earliest guidebooks to Reading, in Freeling's *Great Western Companion* of 1840. The prospectus for this publication makes it clear that George Lovejoy was a fan of the new form of transport:

Railways are now doing for the country what Steam Navigation has done for Sea-Ports and Watering Places, namely pouring in a continual stream of new Visitors; this work therefore holds out great advantages to advertisers, as it will be a book of constant reference, and the companion of all visitors and new residents...The town of Reading, with its peculiar advantages, possesses the means, if properly directed, of becoming one of the most attractive and influential towns in the Kingdom. (*Reading Mercury* 9 November 1839)

He also published *Lovejoy's Almanac*, later *Lovejoy's Household Almanac*, from 1838 until he died. He published maps of Reading and of the country around Reading, and his own edition of the *Register of Facts and Occurrences relating to Literature, the Sciences, and the Arts*. He was prominent in the local Temperance movement and published *The Reading Temperance Messenger and Band of Hope News*.

In 1841, the main Reading Post Office moved to Broad Street, but Lovejoy's was established as a receiving office (and, from 1861, as a money-order office, which we would recognise as a sub-post office). There were two earlier receiving offices in Reading, and later a network around the town. Over time many were closed to be replaced by pillar boxes, but Lovejoy's remained a receiving office for the duration of George Lovejoy's life – another 42 years. On his death the office moved to Duke Street.

In 1835, George Lovejoy put the following notice in the *Reading Mercury*:

The increase of Visitors and Residents in Reading and the neighbour-hood, and the continual applications at the LIBRARY for HOUSES and LODGINGS have suggested the necessity of a GENERAL REGISTER OFFICE for the same:— G. LOVEJOY has, therefore, for the conve-nience of those who have Lodgings &c to let, opened a GENERAL REG-ISTRY, where every information relating to applications for Houses and Apartments, Tenants and Lodgers, may be obtained.——Library, next the Post Office, Reading.' (*Reading Mercury* 28 September 1835)

In this connection his first customer was a Mrs Calder from Chichester, who let 3 Sydney Terrace, the property of a Mrs Stevens. He continued to be what we know as an estate agent for many years.

The selling of patent, or 'quack', medicines had been a feature of the book selling trade in Reading since the days of John Newbery in the eigh-teenth century. George Lovejoy had the Reading franchise for:

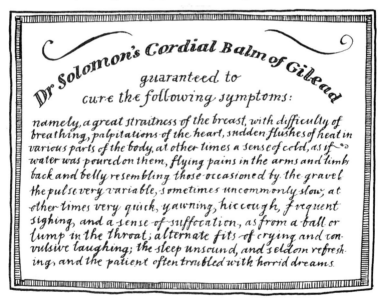

The various London insurance companies had their agents in towns across the country, and for many years, from 1832, George Lovejoy was the Reading agent for the Globe Insurance Company. Outside the world of business, George Lovejoy was active in the broader life of Reading. He ful-filled no elected function, but did serve as a Borough Auditor, where he made a mark by refusing to sign the Accounts on three occasions (1857, 1858, 1864). He campaigned for better public accountability by the publica-tion of properly audited accounts showing 'full information as to how the

money comes in, and how the money goes out.' In this respect, as in others, he was a man ahead of his time.

On 22 September 1840 George Lovejoy hosted a meeting of ten gentlemen of the town (including himself) who met to discuss setting up a Mechanics' Institute 'for the mechanics and other working classes of the town'.

The public rooms built for what became Reading Literary, Scientific and Mechanics Institution are now no. 33 London Street, on the site of Lovejoy's first shop. The foundation stone was laid on 31 August 1842 by Mary Russell Mitford, and the official opening was on 24 October 1843. There had been an earlier incarnation, between 1825 and 1830, but this later establishment was more successful, carrying on its programme of lectures, concerts and other attractions until 1860. Through his connection with the Institute, George Lovejoy came to know many prominent people who visited Reading to give lecture there.

Lovejoy was prominent in the movement which resulted in the acquisition of the Abbey Ruins and Forbury Gardens for the people of Reading. He was also a contributor to the campaign for a Free Library and Reading Rooms in Reading, and was present at the opening of Reading Library on 10 February 1883, a few months before he died. It is fitting that he lived to see the culmination of the Library campaign. He would have made a good Local Studies Librarian – he kept scrapbooks of all sorts of ephemeral information; posters, handbills, newspaper cuttings, business cards, photographs. These are now held in Reading Local Studies Library.

In politics he was a Liberal, and in religion a Baptist. He was a noted campaigner for peace. He visited Paris as part of a British delegation in 1849 (a reciprocal visit after a French delegation had visited London in 1848), and is recalled by Cooper in *Worthies of Reading* thus:

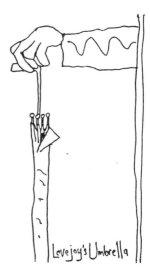

Lovejoy's Umbrella

Some of us remember his placing in his window the large engraving of The Meeting of Wellington and Blucher, to which he appended a card with the apt quotation in large type:

WAR'S A GAME

which, were their subjects wise, Kings would not play at.

George Lovejoy died on 19 July 1883, and his loss was felt far and wide. One comment in particular seems to sum up the general feeling:

It was impossible for anyone to have half-an-hour's conversation with him without perceiving he was no ordinary character: it is not only a family bereavement, but a town and county one.

His funeral was the biggest seen in Reading for many years. Traders in Reading shut their shops as a mark of respect – is there anyone in Reading today who would generate such an action? The great and the good, including both of the town's MPs, followed the cortege to Reading Cemetery.

A contemporary eulogy, printed in the *Reading Observer*, seems an apt conclusion:

To say that George Lovejoy was without his faults and failings would be impious, but we can well afford to write them in water, his good deeds being already written in the memories of many. With his death Reading has lost a landmark. He was unique; an imitation of him is impossible; and it has been well said that by his death, so far as our town is concerned, 'a great book is closed'.

Acknowledgment: I would like to thank Barry de Lacy-Nelson for pointing me in the right direction on numerous occasions.

4:
of yet
more books,
a great fire,
and an evil road

After Lovejoy's death, the Bookshop at no. 39 and its many activities were taken over by Eliza Langley, his assistant for 22 years (she may once have been his fiancee, but the records are discreet).

Miss White continued to run the Post Office at no. 37 after her father's retirement, but stepped down in 1841. By then she had married a prosperous London Street brewer and corn-dealer called John Yard Willats, who ran an Insurance Agency from no. 37 until 1853. The house was bought by George Lovejoy, and became the home of his sister Mary. The ground floor was eventually incorporated into the Bookshop: the front door and windows were removed and replaced by shutters, which survived until 1959.

Fynmore & Jenner's business passed to Thomas Jarman in 1853 when the partnership was dissolved. Jarman disposed of the stock and business to Smith & Son of Duke Street later that year, and the premises at no. 35 became a high-class carpet, upholstery and furniture shop. The proprietor was one Mr Barber, remembered many years later as having been 'a good-looking, very refined man' and a patron of the Mechanics Institute next door. His son Charles Bastin Barber was an artist, trained by Sir Edwin Landseer (of Trafalgar Square lions fame), who went on to work for Queen Victoria.

The old granary in the yard behind no. 35 was demolished in 1841-2 to make way for the Mechanics' Institute, but a warehouse and a stable re-

mained for some years. They were probably demolished by James Banner, who by 1874 was running a Steam Laundry and Dyeing Works (which is curious, since this was more or less the site occupied by another dyer, John Leche, in 1552). 'Damasks Cleaned or Dyed/Chintz Furniture Cleaned and Callendered without unpicking', claimed Banner; 'Ladies' Kid Boots Cleaned or Dyed. Also every description of Furniture and Ladies' and Gentlemens' Wearing Apparel'. The business was taken over by Averell Shillington in 1885 (his name, painted on the brickwork, was still visible on the brickwork within living memory, and was sold again to the Johnson Brothers by 1900.

Although some of the laundry equipment remained in the basement of no. 35 into the 1930s, by 1902 the shop at the front of the building had been let to Dann & Lewis, a well-known firm of Reading photographers. The family of Henry Lewis, a 'dissolving view artist', remained there until 1936. In 1906 they shared the premises with Hedley Brown, bookbinder, printer, picture-framer and artists' colourman.

Eliza Langley

After the demise of Miss Langley in 1897, the Bookshop was sold to William C Long, about whom not much is known. In 1910 he sold the Bookshop to William Smith, a former associate of Lovejoy who had run his own new and second-hand bookshop at no. 97 London Street between 1876 and 1890. The London Street Bookshop was thereafter known as William Smith's until its final closure in 1989. On William's death, the Bookshop was inherited by his son Charles, and, later, by his brother George, who dropped the non-literary side of the business.

Lovejoy's altruistic support for the municipal library service inevitably drew custom away from his own circulating library, but it

※※※ A Famous ※※※ Bookselling Business

Vide **The London "Bookseller," January 20th, 1911.**

survived until the 1930s. It was finally closed down by Wilfred Brown, George Smith's son-in-law, Wilfred Brown, who took over the Bookshop in 1935. Brown developed the antiquarian and second-hand departments instead, and opened branches elsewhere in the town.

He died in 1959, and his successor, Kenneth Adlam, made a number of alterations to the shop, including the rear extension between nos. 35 and 39: 'the glass roof leaked like a sieve whenever it rained', one employee remembers. Things are better now. Adlam, to his credit, made few changes to the old part of the building. He appreciated that the 'atmosphere' of the old building was one of its major charms: 'it would have been all too easy to have left a noisy, tube-lit barn', he told the Evening Post.

Until 1959, the front of no. 37 was open to the elements, with an inset door and shutters. It was rebuilt by the staff: 'no-one would spend any money so when you wanted to change

in the cemetery behind the Friends' Meeting House

things you had to do it yourself', one recalls. Previously threepenny books were on one side of the door, sixpennies on the other and on the pavement outside. Inside was the Education Department, presided over by Mrs Edwards, who worked for the for over thirty years.

The upper floors of no. 37 were let as flats until Adlam took over, when they were converted to shop use. The second floor 'front' contained the staff smoking room and small kitchen, and the attic (with a beautiful stained glass window that probably dates from the era of the Post Office) was the print room. In the disused attic behind no. 39, a model railway, complete with landscaping and tunnels, was installed by David Hutchings, manager of the Secondhand Department: the track ran the full length of the attic.

The Secondhand Department was famous amongst discerning Reading residents. 'It feels like an abandoned library and you're never sure if you're meant to pay for the books at all', wrote the late lamented James Matthews in *Reading Between the Lines*.

Not everyone was pleased with the range of the rest of their stock, however. William Smith's 'occasionally builds up local authors to the extent of displaying a few copies of their books in the window', complained a local author in 1970, 'though not with much more than the enthusiasm of a maiden aunt displaying her underwear'.

In October 1973, the front of the Bookshop was gutted by fire. The Great Fire of London Street was caused by an electrical fault between the first and second floor front of no. 37. David Hutchings, who lived in no. 41, returned home one night along Mill Lane and saw smoke billowing from the Bookshop. 'The fire was fierce and difficult to control because it was raging between the brick walls and wooden cladding of the Victorian building, containing gas pipes, electrics and open gaps in the walls'.

It took six fire engines to put it out; £50,000 of damage was done, although the back of the building was relatively untouched. Some of the tenants, however, were unaware of the fire until the Fire Brigade told them to get out. 'We felt some heat but it wasn't enough to alarm us', the tenant of the flat above the Bookshop told the *Reading Chronicle*. 'It was just as if the weather had changed'. The Bookshop moved into temporary residence down the road into what had been Till's Cafe until the building was restored.

No. 35 was occupied in the 1950s by Barnes & Avis, who at that point sold musical instruments but by 1960 had gotten into servicing televisions instead. By 1968 it was empty, and at some point before 1976 the building was finally acquired by the Bookshop.

Douglas La'Porte was manager of the Bookshop until it closed

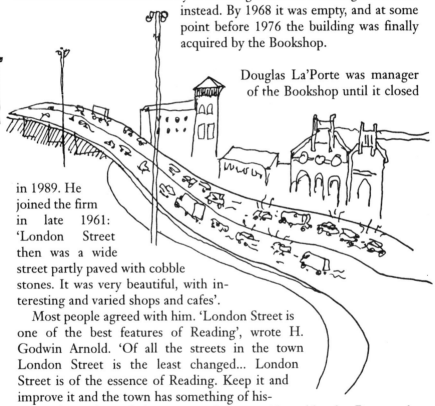

in 1989. He joined the firm in late 1961: 'London Street then was a wide street partly paved with cobble stones. It was very beautiful, with interesting and varied shops and cafes'.

Most people agreed with him. 'London Street is one of the best features of Reading', wrote H. Godwin Arnold. 'Of all the streets in the town London Street is the least changed... London Street is of the essence of Reading. Keep it and improve it and the town has something of historic value and visual pleasure, worth some pride and loyalty. Destroy the street, or let it slowly decay and the town becomes less worth caring for, more a place to get away from'...

Arnold's words were prompted by the infamous Inner Distribution Road, then about to slice across the street. The IDR gives Reading the rare distinction of a ring-road in the town centre: an 'improvement' hatched in the 1960s when people lacking aesthetic appreciation ran the town and old buildings were a nuisance.

It could have been worse. Really. The original plans included a 'motorway box': a road at first floor level, attractively wrapped around London Street, East Street and South Street. This was part of the scheme that would have slashed through the Forbury Gardens and, in one incarnation, demolished the Turks Head in London Road (currently languishing under the brand name of some uppity brewery).

The Council, convinced that this was the best scheme, pronounced itself pleased that the 'amenity' (a contemporary buzz-word) value had been ensured by not actually demolishing the buildings. 'But will they have any meaning in amenity terms when a ramp rises in front of their windows?' asked the *Architect's Journal*.

Of course not. It seems incredible, less than thirty years later, that any sane human could ever have thought otherwise. Public outcry and pressure from all over the country forced the Council's hand, and the 'box' was binned. We now have a nice street-level ring-road instead; though the very existence of the IDR is still an unforgivable blight on Reading's most beautiful thoroughfare.

The IDR cut London Street off from the town centre, and thus doomed many of the street's businesses. It certainly doomed the London Street Bookshop. Blackwell's of Oxford, who took over from Adlam in 1984, at one time considered combining the Bookshop with their shop in Friar Street, but eventually decided to move to new premises opposite the Library in King Street. The move took place in September 1989, to the lamentations of staff and customers alike, and the build-ing stayed empty for six years, when it was acquired by RISC.

5:
of new
beginnings

Reading International Solidarity Centre began life as World Education Berkshire, an educational charity set up by Anne Yarwood – together with others – in 1981. A double-decker bus, colourfully painted with the slogan 'Think Globally – Act Locally', toured schools and community groups from its base at Burnham.

By 1987 it had become clear that WEB needed to have a higher profile in order to be more effective. The charity decided to find a place of its own, and rented 103 London Street. Formerly the Regency art shop, no. 103 possesses 'the best remaining old shopfront' in the street, in the view of Godwin Arnold. (Second-best was no. 39: RISC is a charity with good taste.)

The Council agreed to pay the rent, but the building had been empty for some time, and with only £1,500 to spend on teaching resources and one part-time salary, it took much dedicated voluntary work to get it up and running. Reading International Support Centre finally opened on 17 October 1987, with a meeting room, a fair trade shop and Development Education offices for four WEB workers.

RISC gradually became one of the leading Development Education centres in the country. It soon became clear that RISC needed to move to larger premises, and in 1994, the organisation turned its attention to the seemingly-impossible task of buying the old London Street Bookshop. This is the story of how it all happened, as told by the main RISC team:

Barbara – our resource worker – had a large delivery of books and was frustrated by not being able to put the new books out on the tightly packed shelves. It worried her so much that she couldn't sleep that night. 'There's this big empty building down the road', she thought, 'why don't we rent part of it to increase our

space?' The next morning she told Martin about it, and our search for larger premises nearer the town centre began. We considered the buildings that became 'Pizza Express' and 'Alleycat', but the rents were far too expensive.

Eventually, Martin tracked down the owner of the old London Street Bookshop: Blackwells, and their agent, Mr Thomas of Bristol. It was August 1994 when the builders first unscrewed the door for us. The building seemed enormous and in a desperate state. It had been empty for six years, and had fallen into a state of serious disrepair. The lead roof flashing and copper piping had been looted; broken shelves, papers and pigeon droppings were everywhere. Fires had been lit, and we found tickets for a rave party (entrance fee £5).

It became increasingly clear to us all that we could never afford to rent the place, or even to restore it for use if it was offered rent-free, as we would only become caretakers until the prices went up again. We knew that because property prices had collapsed – in this case from £800,000 to £350,000, including the three flats – that we ought to buy. This was our only chance to move into bigger premises, yet it all seemed an impossible dream. We had developed increasingly firm ideas about how we would use the building – a large fair trade shop, a world cafe, flexible meeting-room

facilities, and office space for like-minded organisations. This would create a dynamic interaction between all these groups. It was all or nothing. We had to raise the money by hook or by crook.

The first step was devising a convincing business plan, so we asked Thames Valley Executive Action for a voluntary financial advisor. They sent us Michael Duerden, a man-in-a-suit who had previously worked for

Coopers & Lybrand. 'I'm here to ask you difficult questions', he said. Painfully, but very diplomatically, he managed to get answers that enabled him to construct a business plan that projected our outgoings and income for the first three years.

We sent it to our own bank who sent it back without reading it and even refused to see us. We then remembered that Mercury Provident – an ethical bank with Quaker roots – had helped Biashara Fair Trade Shop in Bristol, and we submitted our business plan to them. (Mercury Provident was subsequently taken over by Triodos, a Dutch ethical bank). They immediately came to see us, and were encouraging. The first business plan was rejected in April 1995, but after cutting £20,000 off the loan and increasing the revenue, calculating additional running costs, maintenance, depreciation and the rest, our application was finally approved in July. Michael had worked day and night on this, and when we finally got the loan we all celebrated with a bottle of champagne served in plastic cups!

Then came the Herculean task of restoring the building, all 15,000

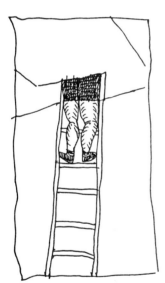

square feet of it! Bente knew Mike McCrae, a community architect in Bristol who had been involved in setting up the Bristol development education centre and understood the issues we were working with. He donated us his time and expertise, enabling us to draw up a feasibility study with a grant from BT Community Architecture Award. He also helped us transform a dark and dingy storeroom (rebuilt after its roof collapsed from dry rot) into an office and a beautiful, light and airy meeting room (nick-named The Stones Room because of the fragments from Reading Abbey found in its walls and now incorporated into its design).

We knew that it was important to time our move so that we would have the proceeds of two Christmases in 15 months to make the repayments on the loan. Resubmitting the business plan caused delays and Blackwells had begun to look for other buyers. However, they were aware that we were serious, and in a depressed property market we provided an opportunity for them to off-load a building that had become a liability. By October 1995, we had managed, as Martin put it, to 'crack the deal'.

The crucial factor was the involvement of Co-op Home Services

(CHS), who took a 999-year lease on the three flats in no 35. CHS and RISC had the active support of Reading Borough Council, who saw the return of residents to London Street as a way to stop its decline. They saw our enterprise as a positive step towards this goal, and helped us in many ways.

We received support from all directions. Chris Keen of CHS offered his time as our surveyor and overseer of the building programme, which included very complex negotiations with Blackwell's surveyor and the building contractors. He too worked weekends on our behalf, and offered to inspect the building once a year to prevent deterioration of the building's fabric.

CHS took possession of the flats in December, but our own completion date was delayed until May 23 1996. We were now faced with the daunting task of completing the building work for the opening in September while organising the One World Tent and Stage for the three-day WOMAD festival in July. Fiona's heroic efforts kept the old shop running during the summer.

It was gruelling work – twelve-hour days, seven day a weeks – directed by the professionals: Steve Hunter the builder, Alan Warner the plasterer, and Ian Harris the electrician and plumber. The spring and summer was bright and sunny with fond memories of sitting in the sun, covered in dust and grime, having tea and lunch perched on planks of wood.

We managed to attract many volunteers to our cause, including two IVS work camps. Ten people came to the first, held in July, and camped out in the RISC office. The next month, eight women came and dossed in what is now the Oxfam Campaigns Office, braving the resident rat, now deceased. These enthusiastic young people from as far afield as Turkey, Spain, Russia and Lithuania gave an invaluable boost to our efforts. Eighteen months later between 200 and 300 volunteers had been involved one way or another. Some reminiscences of that period:

Dave: 'I remember only having a hosepipe from which to get water. Only one electricity supply, with extensions all over the place. The men's toilets stank, but were the first to be restored and were used by all. I remember having to wait for Martin to go away on holiday before tackling the uneven kitchen floor, which was shaped for use as a scullery: the floor curved down to a drain hidden under the concrete. Steve, Ian, Dave and a prisoner, Alf, pouring sweat, hacking up the old floor and re-laying the new one. Grinding the brick walls to allow the plaster to key on to the walls: it was horrendous work, behind a plastic dust sheet. Quarry tiles brought in Ian's car, which struggled up the ramp with the weight. Three days of sore knees laying the tiles and grouting by Jane (Boyd), Bente and a very grumpy Martin.'

Martin: 'My most rewarding experience was working with the young men from the Kennet Unit of Reading Prison. Most of them were all very hard-working, and we developed a close and warm relationship with them and their supervisors. Particularly Chas and the boys working with dedication on the shopfront, sanding, preparing and painting the wood to a very high standard. I remember Steve the builder came initially for one day only to secure the building; eighteen months later he is still with us, having virtually restructured the entire place.'

Barbara: 'I remember Mary coming down from Manchester and spending hour after hour, day after day wire-brushing all the rusty steel girders in the conference room and staying cheerful with music (she had come to have a holiday and some rest!); the early morning call from Pangaea Cafe's John telling us that there was a skip full of carpet tiles at the top of London Street which would be collected by 9.30 that morning – a team of three cars and six people frantically ferrying them down the street to beat the deadline (the tiles now cover the concrete floor in the World Shop); Paul

and Andrew working day and night to unpack and display the crafts in the shop. Andrew posing as a Sixties mannequin with a newly-opened pack of dust sheets.

Fiona: I remember the frantic work of a whole shopful of women carpenters building shelves for display of the fair-traded crafts – buses used to stop outside the shop, with passengers looking on astonished; globe shelves that had been designed by Cathy and built by Paul.

Bente: 'I remember the torturous work of restoring the recycled maple floor for the Conference room. Every single piece of wood had to be scraped free of old varnish, then laid before the start of the International Festival. Pip French was spotted doing 18-hour overnight stints. Then came the gruelling task of sanding and the ten layers of varnish which had to be done over a weekend. I also remember William (Lammas) trying unsuccessfully to line up the lights parallel with the uneven walls; Pip Hall and Suzy Gallina presenting us with a new RISC logo and shopfront design; Pip and Simon Thrower working furiously over the last weekend to finish the signwriting for the front of the building; another race to get the Pangaea Cafe ready in time for the start of the Reading International Festival (with a formal opening by a Buddhist from the Tibet Foundation).

Finally the race to get the shop finished for the September opening and the last minute obstacles. Dry rot re-emerging in the shop and the hallway. Workmen more interested in chatting up the women carpenters than getting rid of the infected wood. Nigel Blake, the demon fire officer telling us, just one week before the opening, to straighten and enclose an open L-shaped staircase from the shop so we had a 'protected' fire escape from the conference room. We couldn't finish the ceiling in the shop because the whole central heating system had to be completed (including the second floor) and tested for leaks before the tiles could be put up. The stories surrounding those hectic months remain fresh in the memory.

Against the odds, RISC (rechristened Reading International Solidarity Centre), moved into the new premises on 16 September. On 19 October the Pangaea Cafe opened for business. The Conference room, three meeting rooms and seven offices were completed over the next few months. A range of local and national organisations, including Oxfam Campaigns Office, One World Week, Reading and Berkshire Refugee Support Group and the illustrious Two Rivers Press, joined RISC in the building. RISC had become the largest Development Education Centre in the country.

What is RISC and what do we do?

RISC is a Development Education centre working with people locally and globally to promote human rights for all and a more equitable distribution of the earth's resources. Development Education is a process which aims to:

- enable people to understand links between their own lives and those of people throughout the world.
- increase awareness of the economic, social, political and environmental forces which shape all our lives, create poverty, inequality and oppression
- develop the skill, attitudes and values which enable people to bring about change and take control of their own lives; and to work towards a more just world, where power and resources are equally shared.

Our mission is nicely summed up in a quote by Elvira Alvarado, a Honduran woman working with peasant communities to obtain basic needs such as land, food, education and health care:

We are not asking for food or clothing or money
We want you with us in the struggle
We want you to educate your people
We want you to organise your people
We want you to join our struggle
Don't be afraid, gringos
Keep your spirits high
And remember
We're right there with you!

We believe that setting up a solidarity centre that enables ourselves and other campaigning groups to work together is an appropriate response to this challenge.

Our team of paid and voluntary workers run a wide range of activities from the centre.

Events

We organise a programme of interactive workshops, feasts, film, art and drama events, exhibitions and provide a platform for speakers from Africa, Asia, South and Central America and the Middle East on issues that are either neglected or marginalised.

Reading International Development Forum

RISC was the prime mover in setting up a Forum – a network of over 80 human rights, environmental and community groups in Reading. In 1988, the Forum organised the first Reading International Festival, now an annual event in the Reading calendar, held during the last two weeks of October. The Forum has so far organised more than 40 different events, from workshops, talk and video screenings to theatre, feasts, music, art and dance.

The Forum also organises the One World Tent and One World Stage at the annual WOMAD (World Of Music Art and Dance) festival, held at Rivermead in Reading. Up to 30 different internationalist groups set up stalls to promote their work, with the stage hosting an exciting mix of world music, talks, workshops, theatre and dance during the three-day event.

The World Shop

The World Shop's trading activities fund the majority of our core running costs. The shop, staffed by a team of volunteers, is open 6 days a week selling a wide range of development education materials, books, fair-traded foods, and crafts as well as environmentally friendly products. It attracts a wide range of peo-

ple who might not otherwise come into contact with development issues as well as supporting farmers and artisans in the South.

Links with Schools

RISC has one of the country's largest selections of development education resources – over 7,000 titles. Our database enables us to respond to requests for information from individuals and organisations. Our Resources Catalogue and subject specific resource lists are distributed to schools, the Youth Service and community organisations and we provide resource displays and in-service training to schools throughout Berkshire. Our mail order service is used by customers from as far afield as Japan, Australia and Canada. A loan service of anti-racist resources has been established in what was Lovejoy's Lending Library. Early in 1998 we will set up another loan service of artefacts illustrating the diversity of people's lives, from Kenya, Nigeria and St Lucia – and later from India and Pakistan.

Focus for Change

Focus for Change is the publications arm of RISC. We produce teaching/campaigning resources in collaboration with local, national and international partners. We have published teaching packs and laminated exhibitions with organisations from Nepal, the Philippines, Kenya, Germany, Italy and Belgium. Voluntary workers contribute research and writing time. Recent publications and exhibitions include:

- Focus for Change – gender, race and class inequality and the media in an international context;

- Taking Responsibility: Internationalist Anti-Sexist Youth Work for Young Men;

- Human Rights for All? – a global view of lesbian and gay oppression;

- XChanging the World: looks at how the world trading system is unsustainable because it is increasing inequality and environmental and social destruction, in both North and South;

- China Through Women's Eyes: photos and text reflecting on the rapid changes which are taking place in China and challenge many of the stereotypes we have;

- Worlds Behind the Music: puts the music produced by artists in the South into a wider social and political context.

Centre Facilities

RISC offers conference and meeting room facilities to voluntary and statutory organisations, as well as individuals, with special rates for charities and voluntary groups. Over 80 different organisations, including Greenpeace, Friends of the Earth and Amnesty, make use of the Centre. They can finish their meeting with a drink and food in Pangaea World Cafe.

The Future

Now that the main fabric of the building has been completed, the centre offers infinite possibilities for the future. We dream of finding more innovative ways to promote understanding of global issues: a rolling programme of performance poets, book launches, craft workshops, story-telling for adults, themed banquets...the sky's the limit. Realising these dreams depends on the continuing enthusiasm of our local community, without whom we wouldn't be here today.

RISC is an educational charity registered as World Education Berkshire (No 293799) and a Company Limited by guarantee (No 1987368)

RISC is run collectively by workers and a voluntary management committee. We are funded with income from the shop, donations, membership subscriptions and grants from Oxfam Christian Aid, Reading Borough Council, the European Union and the National Lottery.

For more information contact:

Reading International Solidarity Centre
35-39 London Street
Reading RG1 4PS
Tel 0118 958 6692 Fax 0118 959 4357
Email risc@gn.apc.org
Website http://www.gn.apc.org/risc

appendix: a mysterious presence in the attic

London Street has always been popular with ghosts. Perhaps they feel at home amongst all those old buildings.

An ancient shoemakers' shop on the South Street corner was rumoured to be haunted in the 1870s. 'I have seen crowds of people packed into South Street and all down London Street on more than one occasion drawn thereto by the report that a 'ghost' was to be seen', recalled John Luther Hawking. An eminent local doctor 'tried to persuade the people that it was all humbug, and offered to stay there all night to prove it'. Whether he did so or not we do not know, but no more was heard of that particular ghost.

No. 39 London Street, however, has a well-attested phantom. Over to Leslee Hopper:

> Many people sensitive to the presence of spirits have mentioned feeling a presence in certain areas of the building, mostly on the stairs up to the office from the shop, in the notoriously cold passageway outside the photocopy room (where Major Redway had his sighting), in the photocopy room itself, and in the attic area, where the builders had their experience. Everyone has expressed that it is a comfortable feeling, 'one of calmness'; another said that the ghost sees his role as 'caretaker' – 'he's looking after the place'.
>
> It hasn't been easy trying to get information for this section of the book, as a lot of people who did see the ghost have died, so the information we have used is second-hand. It was because of this that I decided to ask a medium friend of mine if he would interview the ghost. We had a brief visit in the rooms above the office area where Rhys, the medium, confirmed there was a man here. Rhys asked if we could come back and talk to him another time and 'the man' agreed.
>
> Rhys returned at the appointed time: three other people were present.

The 'ghost' gave his name as John Ascott or Ashcroft, in 1826 aged 34 years, who rented lodgings there. He was very strongly related to a Christian movement but it wasn't his faith; he held meetings in the meeting house for 17 years (Quaker meetings?) and died from consumption in the room above the photocopy room.

Neither John Ascott nor John Ashcroft have yet cropped up as names in any other context, but a humble lodger of the 1820s may well have eluded all the records. Consumption was certainly on the increase at that date: George Lovejoy's first wife died from it in 1837.

The preferred identity, amongst employees, was always William Penn. 'Whenever a book, order form or other important document went missing, the cry would often be heard: 'Old Bill's taken it!', remembers Martin J Horne.

Major Ernest Redway, formerly of the Indian Army, had worked in the second-hand department since the war. He was one of the first people to see the ghost, as David Hutchings, who later managed the department, told Leslee Hopper:

In the autumn of 1958, Major Redway came down from the area where the ghost had been seen, one day very excited and said 'I've seen William Penn!' What he actually saw was a Quaker gentleman whom he described as wearing the style of hat that was worn, in a shaft of sunlight in the old passageway; he saw the image through a small window that was in the passage.

He wasn't the sort of guy who had fanciful thoughts and certainly the one person I would believe that he saw something. No doubt about it, he was really quite excited and pleased about it.

We had a number of people working there who couldn't work in the room, particularly above the old passageway. Jim Sporry, whom I took over from, he went up there and said, 'I just can't work up in that room, there's something up there, I'm not alone!' That was in 1957 before I arrived; he told that to Mrs Edwards who was then in charge of our depart-

ment. I actually talked to Jim Sporry about it and I believe him. Another young chap, Keith Ewers, had the same problem.

We often got Americans coming in to see the garden where William Penn was alleged to have sat during his last years. They would also ask to see the ghostly attic, which was not too difficult to arrange as it was still in use as part of the second-hand bookshop, where Biographies were kept, separated by a wall from the rest of the attic and only accessible from the present photocopying room. Major Redway used to take them up and tell them his story of the sighting.

The passageway where Major Redway had the sighting I must say was always icy cold even when it was 90 degrees outside. I was taken with the fact that as soon as you went through the door to that area you'd hit an ice-box.

My wife worked in the small office, the small office that is now the photocopying room as I understand it. She would walk out of her office, which was normal temp', into the passageway outside which was always quite cold. Everybody at the time agreed that it was a cold spot. And to this day it still is.

Lindsay Green is one of many Reading people to have been thrilled by the knowledge that the London Street Bookshop was haunted. 'It must have been about twenty years ago that my elder sister and I would gladly leave the dentist and walk the short distance to the London Street Bookshop. As a reward for good behaviour we were allowed to roam around the Bookshop and look at whichever books we pleased. One feeling always surpassed the initial thrill of my new-found freedom however, and this was the knowledge that roaming somewhere on a staircase not too far from the children's department was 'a real live ghost'! Of course I never actually saw the ghost, but this fact never dampened the mysterious excitement a trip to the London Street Bookshop aroused in me.'

The most recent 'sighting' occurred during the summer of 1996. Two builders who were working on the renovations had occasion to sleep in the office area of the new RISC building. They were woken by loud banging, 'like the sound of a wall being knocked through', they said. The noise was coming from the attic rooms above the office area, and they bravely made their way up the stairs into the attic. When they got up there they actually saw a figure of a man, which disappeared through the wall. They were visibly shocked and the 'figure' disappeared. They ran out of the building and waited outside until Cumbers cafe opened at 7.30, still very shaken by their experience.

bibliography

In the Berkshire Record Office:
Poor Rate Books, 1745-1846 (on microfilm)
D/EBy f 71 (Saunders' 1813 Act of Parliament)
D/A1/100/157c (will of Richard Minns, 1785)
D/Ey f6 (Fynmore & Jenner bills)

In the Reading Local Studies Library (bracketed letters indicate shelf-marks):

Manuscripts and Newspapers
Reading Mercury and *Berkshire Chronicle*
Clarke, Muriel street index cards for London Street
Hawking, John Luther *Reminiscences of Reading* n.d. (19 nn) R/DX
Cuttings file, London Street and William Smith's

Books and articles
'A Famous Business' in *The London Bookseller* 20.1.1911. R/JO
Man, John *The Stranger in Reading* 1810. R/IB
Alexander, Alan *Borough Government and Politics* 1985. R/F
Anderson, Arthur Henry *Reading and its surroundings* 1906-7. R/CV
Arnold, H G *Report on London Street, Reading* n.d. (?1966). R/NK
As Stupid as Oxen; a history of the Reading and Silchester Methodist circuit (1988). q R/LJ
Astill, G 'Reading' in (ed) *Historic Towns in Berkshire*. qB/DA
Burden, Eugene *Printed Maps of Berkshire 1574-1900*. Typescript. qB/UX
Part 2 *Town Plans* 1994.
Part 3 *Environs and District maps 1607-1900* 1995.
Burton, K G *The early Newspaper Press in Berkshire (1723-1855)* Typescript. 1954. B/UX
Childs, W M *Reading during the early part of the nineteenth century* 1910. R/DX
Childs, W M 'Reading in the Seventeenth Century', in *University College*

Review 1914. R/KM

Cooper, John James *Worthies of Reading* 1923. R/TA

Corley, T.A.B. 'The Earliest Reading Bank: Marsh, Deane and Co', in *Berkshire Archaeological Journal* 66 (1971-72), pp. 121-9. B/DA

Crawfurd, Gibbs Payne *The registers of the parish of St Mary's, Reading, Berks 1537-1812* 1891. R/TQD

(Darter, William Silver) *Reminiscences of Reading* 1889. R/DX

Deloney, Thomas *Thomas of Reading* 1612 (reprinted 1969). R/TU/CoL

Dils, Joan (ed.) *Redding 1540-1640: A Portrait of a Community* n.d. (?1981). R/DT

Ditchfield, P H (ed.) *Reading Seventy Years Ago* 1887. R/DX

Dormer, E *Gray of Reading* 1923. R/TU/GRA

Fernyhough's Reading Directory 1841. R/CY

Freeling, A *Great Western Railway Companion* 1840. BX/NQ

Goose, N R 'Decay and Regeneration in seventeenth-century Reading: a study in a changing economy' in *Southern History* 6 (1984) pp 53-74. qR/IA

Harman, L.W. *History of Christianity in Reading.* R/LA

Harman, L.W. *A History of Education in Reading.* Typescript. 1960 p41/42. R/KA

Harman, L.W. *The Parish of St Giles in Reading* 1946. R/LB

Higgs, Edward *Making sense of the census* 1989 929.3

Historic Manuscripts Commission, *11th Report* part 7 1888. R/ED

Homer-Wooff, G.H.R. & Jones, Peter J. *Postal History of Reading* Pts 1 & 2 1981 & 1982. R/HN

In Memoriam George Lovejoy 1884. R/TU/LOV

In Memoriam MJL; Funeral Sermon preached at Reading on September 14 1856...upon the occasion of the death of Martha Jane Lovejoy. R/TU/LOV

Ingall's *Directory for Reading and its vicinity* 1837. R/CY

Kemp, Brian (ed.) *Cartularies, Reading Abbey* 1986 & 1987. R/LE

Lovejoy, George *First visit to Boulogne & Paris* 1849 Scrapbook, 1849. qR/TU/LOV

Lovejoy's *Almanac and Appendix for the year 1849.* R/UX

Lovejoy's *Household Almanack and Year Book of Useful Knowledge for 1877.* R/UX

Macaulay's *Reading Directory, Almanac and Official Register for 1859.* R/CY

Man, John *The History and Antiquities of the Borough of Reading* 1816. QR/D

Matthews, J (ed.) *Reading Between the Lines*, 1988. R/CV

Phillips, Daphne ed. *Reminiscences of Reading: an Octogenarian* 1985. R/DX

Post Office *Directory of Berkshire* 1847 (Kelly). B/CY

Post Office *Reading Directory* 1842 (Snare). R/CY

Preston, A G 'The Demolition of Reading Abbey' in *Berks Archaeological Journal* 39 (1935). B/DA

Roberts, W.J. (*Notebook on Lovejoy*). R/TU/LOV

S Giles, Reading. *Complete list of Monumental Inscriptions in the churchyard as they are in 1926* Manuscript, 1926. B/TQF

Slade, C L 'Reading' in M. Lobel (ed.) *Historic Towns* (1969). fR/D

Watts, AT *The Foundation and Development of the Reading Mechanics' Institution 1825-1830 and 1840-1860* Typescript, 1976. qR/RK

Wykes, Alan *Reading 1970.* R/D

Yorke's *Reading Street Key* 18 January 1839. R/CY

and finally, courtesy of the London Street Research Group:

London Street Described: a Reading historical record 1800-1900 (their forthcoming publication, which gives details of all nineteenth-century householders and much more besides).

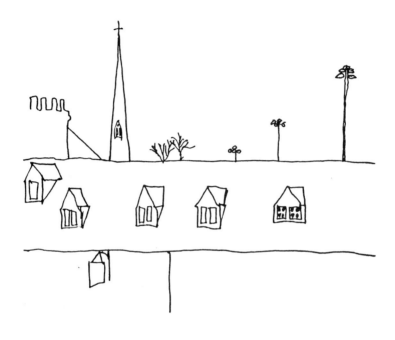

view from two rivers press' office